2024 New Year's Resolutions Time:

Say No to Failed Resolutions and Learn the Secret to Making Realistic and Keeping New Year's Resolutions

By

Charles Morales

Table of Contents

New Year Resolution Time

Chapter One 6

Introduction 6

Chapter Two 10

When and Why?...10

Why Do People Make New Year's Resolutions.....................10

When Did New Year's Resolutions Begin? 11

The Power of The New Year's Resolution 13

Why Do New Year's Resolutions Fail?................................15

Chapter Three 20

Setting New Year Resolutions in Context: The Personal Change Process 20

Making Personal Change: Developing New Habits.................21

The Science of Developing Habits.....................................22

The Importance of Development Mentality 27

Chapter Four 30

How to Make New Year's Resolutions 30

How Can I Make a Realistic New Year's Resolution That Will Work?..32

How To Stick to New Year's Resolutions............................37

Guidelines for Effective New Year's Resolutions 39

Crucial Elements..47

What Are the Best New Year's Resolutions? 48

Chapter Five 52

Resolution Ideas For 2024..52

Boost Your Goals for The New Year...................................53

Ideas for New Year's Resolutions and How to Achieve Them ...55

Chapter Six 56

Self-Improvements for a Better You for the New Year.............56

Conclusion..86

Chapter One

Introduction

My life revolves around New Year's resolutions just as much as it does around festivities. My goal for the new year is to be proud of myself and impart knowledge or other things to people. For me, making new year's resolutions is crucial, as I need to have a purpose or objective. I also wish to fulfill some of the resolutions from the new year. At year's end, I made a pledge to myself to do just that. I'm having fun as I make new objectives and reflect on my missteps from the past.

We've all undoubtedly made at least one New Year's resolution in the past, driven by the desire to start over. But by January 31st, how many of us can really claim that we are still adhering to our resolutions? It seems likely that the answer is very few—and fewer still by the end of the year.

Making ambitious statements is all very well, but genuine personal change takes commitment. This book explains how you can make more realistic New Year resolutions to give you a much better chance of keeping them and delivering real change in your life.

It's a new year and a moment to commit to and approach the future with courage, getting your desired job, being more creative, becoming fitter and healthier, and spending more time with your family. You may achieve these and many more objectives just like them.

Undoubtedly, some resolutions have been sidetracked by the "Curse of the New Year Resolution." It need not, however, end with yours.

Thus, unwind and make a commitment to achieving your New Year's goals. I'll be discussing how to lay the groundwork for an amazing future in this book.

Many people worldwide believe that a new year is a good opportunity for a fresh start, and they often celebrate this decision by setting resolutions for the next year. Nonetheless, certain statistics indicate that over 50% of resolutions end in failure. Here, we examine how you might achieve your objectives by making long-lasting adjustments.

We'll look at some examples of New Year's resolutions, why people break them, how to create your own, and how to keep to them. Get ready to put your best foot forward.

New Year Resolution Time

Chapter Two

When and why?

Why Do People Make New Year's Resolutions?

To many, there is a certain appeal to making a change at the start of the new year. New beginnings often signal a time for a fresh start—a chance to put past mistakes behind and look to the future.

Having an entire year ahead can feel like a blank slate, full of opportunity and potential. When individuals make significant adjustments for the next year, they also have a feeling of control.

Tradition has a part as well. As we'll see, there is a specific cultural component for certain individuals since resolutions have been made for many generations.

But because of all of these elements, individuals are often under a lot of pressure to make these adjustments, which may be one of the causes of the high failure rate.

When Did New Year's Resolutions Begin?

The first known references to New Year's resolutions come from the ancient Babylonians. The Babylonians celebrated the beginning of the new year and the sowing of crops as long as 4,000 years ago. In an attempt to win the gods' favor, they pledged to repay debts and return any valuables they had borrowed while reaffirming their allegiance to the monarch.

History also shows us that the Romans had similar practices, and they eventually moved the calendar around so the year started on January 1st. This coincided with the celebration of the god Janus, who looked back on the previous year and looked ahead to the future. The Romans made promises of good conduct for the year ahead.

While the idea of setting goals for the next year is mostly associated with the West, other cultures follow comparable customs. For example, in Japan, some people practice Kakizome, where they write their goal for the year ahead in ornate calligraphy.

Even with their archaic origins, a lot of individuals still make goals every year. For example, according to one survey, 44% of people in the UK planned on making resolutions every year.

The Power of The New Year's Resolution

As the holidays approach and the New Year approaches, many individuals are thinking back on the past and reevaluating some of their choices. For those who haven't started making the changes they promised to start next week, next month, or maybe when winter arrives, the New Year's resolutions provide the ideal chance. We'll share fascinating details regarding this resolution with you in this post and provide helpful suggestions for coming up with a winning list of objectives for the next year.

Nowadays, 45% of Americans make New Year's resolutions. While nearly half of all Americans make resolutions, 25% of them give up on their resolutions by the second week of January.

New Year's resolutions vary around the world. Or at least, that's the conclusion you could draw from Google Maps project called Zeitgeist. Internet users from around the world were invited to share their resolutions. Google then mapped and evaluated them, classifying them into the following domains: education, money, profession, love, and health.

Looking at the map, health-related resolutions predominated in the US and Egypt. Visitors from Australia and Japan were looking for love. In Russia, meanwhile, education was the top priority. And in India, career goals were dominant.

Of course, this is far from a scientific study, but it's still interesting.

So, what were the top New Year's resolutions? Social attempted to answer that question based on users' tweets. Here are the results:

- Save money

- Be a nicer human.

- Get a new job.

- Give more time and money to charity.

- Drink less

- Diet, exercise, and weight loss

- Read more

- Learn something new.

- Sleep more

- Make new friends

Why Do New Year's Resolutions Fail?

Examining the reasons why it might be difficult for you to maintain your New Year's goals is one technique to help you understand how to make resolutions that you are likely to stick to.

These include:

1. You weren't really motivated to achieve your goals since you weren't that interested in doing so. This is often the case with New Year's resolutions, since they are typically actions we feel we should do rather than ones we like, not that we want to do. Goals have to excite and motivate you, or you simply won't achieve them.

2. Your goals were too ambitious; you may have struggled to know where to start or simply given up in despair at the size of the task.

3. Your goals focused on processes, not outcomes. It is much easier to motivate ourselves to do something if we think about the outcome we want to achieve, not what we have to do to get there. For instance, it's much simpler to save a little bit more when you consider the purpose of your savings—perhaps purchasing a home or a vehicle.

4. Your goals did not advance you toward a more comprehensive "life goal." You could not see how they were going to help you get to where you really wanted to be in life.

5. The timing of your goal was not defined, so there was no incentive to get started. We often need some kind of 'kick-start' for personal change, and a time-bound goal can help.

6. You didn't pause to consider the actions you would need to take in order to accomplish your objectives. Having a clear idea of what you need to do is essential.

A fast search on the internet will provide a variety of statistics on the failure rate of resolutions. Whatever the result, it's usually pretty high. So why are people so bad at completing their yearly goals?

There are a few potential reasons:

- The aims aren't specific enough. It's really easy to be unclear while making resolutions. 'Eat less chocolate' or save more money' aren't particularly goal-focused or measurable. What does more or less look like? And over what time period? Finding the right problem to solve can be helpful.

- There are too many resolutions. Many people go too far with the idea of a new start, compiling a list of their own imagined crimes and attempting to atone for each one. As soon as one goes by the wayside, it can be disheartening to continue with the others.

- It's hard to change behaviors. Ultimately, New Year's resolutions are usually about changing behaviors. If you don't recognize them and alter the mentality that fuels them, it may be challenging to do so.

- There's no accountability. It's not always easy to be self-accountable. Individuals are skilled at offering justifications or overlooking little mistakes. People rarely hold their goals up to others to keep them accountable.

It should, therefore, be clear that setting the right resolutions or goals is an essential part of being able to keep your New Year resolutions.

Chapter Three

Setting New Year Resolutions in Context: The Personal Change Process

Any process of personal growth goes through these stages:

1. Establishing your own objectives and vision: deciding where you want to go in life.

2. Organizing your personal growth involves determining the steps necessary to achieve your objectives and vision.

3. Starting to make changes: actually, doing something to move towards your goals.

4. Evaluating your learning in order to determine what you have accomplished and what more needs to be done.

5. Revising your plan if necessary to reflect your progress and even changes to your vision and goals as a result of the reality of making changes.

In essence, New Year's resolutions are just personal aspirations or visions of who you want to be in the future. As such, they are just a portion of the process of bringing about personal development.

Although they constitute the beginning, they are insufficient on their own. There is also an art and a science to setting a personal vision and goals— and if you do not make them appropriate, you will not find them motivating enough to keep!

Making Personal Change: Developing New Habits

But what about when you think you have made the right resolutions? You began, you were driven, and you established time limitations, but why couldn't you find enough time?

Is there anything you can do about that? The answer is yes—and it lies in understanding how we develop new habits (see box). It also entails continuing your commitment while accepting the odd slip-up.

The Science of Developing Habits

The adage "practice makes perfect" is not new.

Few of us ever actually attain perfection, but there is no question that practice is essential to developing any new skill. It turns out that practice is essential to developing any new habit, too.

Research shows that we need to do something for about 20 hours before it becomes a habit.

This is just a general "rule of thumb," not an absolute: certain people and habits take longer to form, while others can do it more rapidly. However, you should not expect to develop any new habits without putting in this kind of time. In other words, if you only go to the gym once a week, you can expect it to take a good few months before it becomes a habit.

Once you understand that it takes a good 20 hours to develop a new habit, it becomes clear that you have to do something regularly for quite a while before it will become second nature.

It is because it is not yet a habit that makes it difficult to start anything new and fit it into your day.

You therefore have to work much harder at it for the first few weeks, especially if you don't do it very often, because you have not yet 'hard-wired' it into your brain. You have to think about it consciously and make time for it, or it won't happen.

If you put this together with setting good goals, you have a much better chance of making New Year's resolutions that will actually work.

Worked example: "I will go to the gym once a week next year."

Suppose that you decide that you want to go to the gym once a week. Let's pick that apart and see how that can be made easier to achieve.

- **Focus on outcomes**. You don't actually want to go to the gym once a week. You want to feel better and be more physically fit. You may even want to be eligible to compete in a specific event, like a swim or fun run. This can be helpful because it also sets a time limit and makes sure that you will keep going. This is therefore much more motivating.

- Make it precise. You are going to the gym one day per week—but when exactly? It can be more convenient if you say that you will do the task "once a week" as opposed to "on a specific morning before work." If you wait until Friday, you might discover that you have not completed the task. You will also find that blocking out a particular morning is easier because both you and other people will get used to it and will stop trying to fill that space in your diary.

- Keep going—and don't worry if you occasionally miss a session. The key to developing a new habit is to keep going. Inform others and ask them to support you as well. If you are unable to visit the gym one week, don't worry too much; just go the next week (or even go twice the next week). The secret is to persevere, as this will guarantee that it gets ingrained. If you really find it difficult, consider scheduling a personal training session or making plans to see a buddy; these arrangements will make it much simpler to find the time when you would otherwise have to disappoint someone.

- Monitor advancement. While it's not required, using a fitness tracker might help you see your progress. Merely assessing your abilities or the number of weeks you have made it to the gym may serve as an excellent means of monitoring your growth.

- Give yourself a reward when you succeed. Remember to celebrate your accomplishments! If, after a few weeks, you haven't succeeded in your New Year's goals, it's crucial to persevere.

- Personal development is very much a marathon, not a sprint. Realistic and worthwhile goals take time to achieve but may lead to lifelong changes. They are worthwhile endeavors that require a lot of effort.

The Importance of Development Mentality

Possessing a development mentality is perhaps one of the most crucial components of achieving a New Year's goal. Let's take a definition from our open step on study strategies if you're not sure what it entails.

"Having a growth mindset increases your belief in your own ability to succeed and, consequently, your actual chance of success."

Those with a fixed mindset see their strengths and weaknesses as part of who they are as a person. As a result, they're more likely to seek out opportunities where they can demonstrate their strengths and avoid situations that might expose their weaknesses.

Studies have also shown that those with a fixed mindset are more likely to quit when facing hurdles and setbacks because they don't feel they have the natural ability to succeed.

On the other hand, those with a growth mindset believe that they can learn and grow. They recognize that effort, careful planning, and ongoing learning can all outweigh natural ability when it comes to achieving success.

A growth mindset acknowledges that steady advancement is possible with effort. It also means seeing mistakes and failures as opportunities to learn and seeking out opportunities to challenge themselves to do better.

When it comes to sticking to New Year's resolutions, this type of growth mindset can be a huge help.

Chapter Four

How to Make New Year's Resolutions

Now let's pay attention to setting our own resolutions for the next year. First, let's go back to effective goal-setting to get started.

There are five principles of goal-setting:

- They should be clear.
- They should provide a motivating amount of challenge.
- They should have the commitment of the person setting them
- Feedback on progress should be taken into account.
- The complexity of the required tasks should be taken into account.

So, going back to one of the 'best' examples outlined above, let's turn it into a more meaningful one—exercise more.

Rather than using the comparatively general phrase, let's first define it. An adult's recommended amount of exercise is at least 150 minutes of moderate aerobic activity or 75 minutes of vigorous aerobic activity a week. This is a good starting point.

Let's now quantify and achieve it: in January, engage in at least 150 minutes a week of moderate exercise. Once again, there are many methods to monitor your development in this area, and the first time frame is really brief.

Your resolution also needs to be relevant to your life, so you may have a bigger goal in mind. For example, you might challenge yourself to complete a 10-kilometer run by April. This provides you with a concrete timeline and the opportunity to go closer to your objective, step by step.

By building your resolution this way, you can have a clear goal with a motivating amount of challenge. You're also showing commitment to the resolution by giving a firm date and allowing the chance for feedback on your progress in case you need to adjust.

How Can I Make a Realistic New Year's Resolution That Will Work?

Almost 30% of people never make New Year's resolutions because they know they will not be able to keep them. On the other hand, those who set resolutions for the New Year have a tenfold higher chance of succeeding than those who don't.

A solid strategy might assist you in resolving a variety of issues. It can also help make your life exactly the way you want it to be. But making a plan is not always an easy task. Therefore, we have prepared some detailed tips for you.

1. **Summarize The Past Year**

Possessing the proper mindset is the first step towards good planning. Take out your favorite pen and notepad, sit down, and evaluate the last year in terms of your successes, setbacks, and new contacts.

If you also made a New Year's resolution the previous year, be sure to include it here.

If you also made a New Year's resolution the previous year, be sure to include it here. How many goals have you reached? Why haven`t you been able to implement other goals? If you have been setting the same goal for yourself for a few years but still cannot make it come true, perhaps you don't really need it, and the goal is imposed by the environment or advertising.

2. Define The Concept of The Year

Before you begin the in-depth planning, it would be excellent if you could clearly state your one primary objective for the year. Also, before setting any goal, make sure that this is exactly what you really want. It corresponds to your interests and desires.

3. Break Down Goals into Small Tasks

Try to test every goal with the questions. Below, you can find examples:

- ***If the goal is not met, what will happen?***
- ***What am I willing to pay to fulfill it (time, effort)?***

- *What am I improving in myself and in the world by achieving this goal?*

If the goal is really crucial, then break it down into specific tasks. For convenience, you can divide them into six conditional lists: "work," "family," "relationships," "money," "interests," and "personal development.".

To make sure your goals are clear and reachable, you can use the SMART methodology. It states that each of them ought to be:

- *Specific (simple, sensible, significant).*
- *Measurable (meaningful, motivating).*
- *Achievable (agreed, attainable).*
- *Relevant (reasonable, realistic, and resourced; results-based).*
- *Time-bound (time-based, time-limited, time/cost-limited, timely, time-sensitive)*

4. Make a Plan For a Plan

Timely distribution of the subtasks is the first step towards starting implementation. We suggest making lists of tasks for the month, week, and day with periodic reminders. You can use planner apps for smartphones, Google Calendar, paper lists, etc.

Of course, you won't be able to plan the whole year by the hour, but it is a feasible task to outline a general plan and periodically return to it for clarifications.

5. Believe in Yourself

"Whether you think you can or you think you can't, you're right."

Belief in yourself and your capabilities is one of the main secrets of success. Take another look at your list of future accomplishments this year. Do you really believe you can do it?

How To Stick to New Year's Resolutions

Of course, just because you've got a solid resolution doesn't mean that you're automatically going to succeed. As with many changes in life, it takes time and effort to see the results. In what way, then, can you maintain your New Year's resolutions?

When it comes to maintaining your goals, there are a few things to keep in mind. Here are a few easy wins:

Remain tenacious. While it may seem apparent, persistence is key to moving forward in any endeavor. Missing a day or failing to meet a milestone doesn't mean that you've failed; it just means you have to try again tomorrow. You have to keep motivated.

Be consistent. Similarly, finding a routine to follow can help you persist. Fitting in regular time in your schedule to work towards your goal means that it becomes a habit, and you can take gradual steps.

Learn as you go. You may find that your initial resolution isn't quite right. It could be too easy, too hard, or not practical with your current situation. It's proper to take these lessons to heart and modify your goals accordingly.

Inform others. You may hold your resolutions more accountable by sharing your aspirations with others. You may let those closest to you know that you're working toward certain objectives without having to provide specifics. Then, if you need assistance, they may provide it.

Guidelines for Effective New Year's Resolutions

This guideline for the new year's resolutions will help you get off to a successful start.

First Rule: Stick to Your Decision

A strong will to change is the first step toward successful resolutions. In order to succeed, you have to have faith in your ability to complete the tasks at hand. Thus, as you establish them, bear the following in mind:

- Make sure your resolutions are constructive and ones you really want to fulfill.

- Tell everyone you know about your resolve, and they will assist in keeping you responsible.

- Create a ritual to initiate your commitment; this will help it seem more "real" and meaningful to you.

- Don't wait until the last minute to choose your resolution.

- Give your objectives some thought. You run the danger of ignoring the bigger picture and just responding to your immediate surroundings if you don't.

- Is this my idea or someone else's? These are some questions you should ask yourself to see whether you can accept responsibility for your goal.

- Does this resolve give me a sense of purpose and energy?

- Is this resolve in line with my long-term goals and beliefs, among other aspects of my life?

- Recall that accomplishing your goal doesn't have to take the whole year.

Advice:

One effective method for encouraging you to stick with your objectives or aspirations is visualization. Consider what it would be like to reach your objective. In what way are you feeling? How are you? How do other people see you?

By seeing yourself in the role you want, you may increase your drive and confidence in your ability to succeed. For further information, see our page on visualization.

Rule 2: Maintain Realism

- Motivation is essential for reaching objectives. But if you hold yourself too high, you run the danger of failing.

- Be very cautious not to make the same resolution as you did the previous year. If it did not work back then, you must ensure that there is a solid basis for your belief that this year will bring it about. What has altered?

- Instead of aiming too high, aim down. Strive for a difficult goal that you have a decent probability of achieving.

- Aim no larger than you can chew. You should not make more than one or two resolutions. If you do more, you will be dividing your attention and effort.

Rule 3 Put It in Writing

Make a written resolution. It's an easy, but effective, way to bring your vision to life. When we take the time to accomplish this, there is something within us that reacts with more fervor and dedication. Think about putting it down on index cards and placing it in a visible location. like on your refrigerator, desk, or wallet, for instance.

Rule 4: Create a Schedule

- Don't skip this step; it's really crucial!
- Start by putting yourself in the desired situation.
- After that, trace your route back to your current location.
- Jot down every milestone that has to be met in between.
- Make a plan for achieving each of these objectives. Every step must be understood, and you must prepare for the following move.

Rule 5: Show Flexibility

Not every scenario will unfold exactly as you had envisioned. The smallest little impediment might derail you, especially if your approach is overly strict. Thus, maintain your adaptability and flexibility by doing the following:

Try to foresee some of the difficulties you may encounter. As you mentally get ready for the others, make a backup plan for the ones that have the biggest chance of failing.

Acknowledge the possibility that your resolve may evolve over time. That's reality, not failure. Make whatever necessary adjustments to the aim in order to keep pursuing it.

It's not a hard-and-fast rule that demands resolutions be made in January. Wait until March; if your situation dictates, that would be preferable.

Rule 6: Make Notes

- If you have a lot of other commitments, duties, and obligations, it may be difficult to stay focused on your strategy. To maintain your resolve, create a structured reminder system. To do this, keep the following things in mind:

- Make your written goals available. Place reminders on your calendar, in your briefcase, in the vehicle, at work, at home, and so on.

- Verify that your to-do list includes the scheduled tasks.

- Set your desktop calendar to remind you of the tasks you need to do in order to reach your objectives.

Rule 7: Monitor Development

- It is important for you to recognize when each milestone is reached because the satisfaction you get from little victories will inspire you to keep going.

- Keep a diary and consistently record your improvements in it.

- Write down the moments when you were very happy with your work.

- Keep a journal of your low points and suicidal thoughts.

- Regularly review your entries to gain knowledge from your experiences.

- Talk about your development with loved ones, friends, or coworkers.

Rule 8: Reward Yourself

- Sometimes a tiny gift or reward is the best way to give someone who is already very devoted a boost!

- While creating your strategy, list some objectives that you want to reach and treat yourself to when they are. Spread them apart, however, to ensure that the prizes stay unique and difficult to get.

Crucial Elements

Make or break your New Year's resolutions. You get to make the decision. You could decide not to set resolutions ever again if they hurt. Decide now to make it enjoyable!

Focusing on something you are ready to fully dedicate yourself to and that you really desire is the first step. If you follow through on this, you'll have a wonderful foundation for success and motivation!

Use these eight guidelines to ensure that your New Year's resolutions are as successful as you intend them to be.

What Are the Best New Year's Resolutions?

Finding the 'best' resolution is, of course, an entirely subjective process. It is possible that what works for you will not work for others, and vice versa. A helpful place to start is by figuring out what success means to you.

As we'll see, there are several things you can do to make your New Year's resolutions as beneficial as possible. To set effective goals, you should:

- Be specific
- Set measurable and attainable milestones.
- Make them relevant to your life.
- Give firm timescales to achieve them.

Essentially, you want to outline exactly what you want to achieve and when you want to achieve it, ensuring that you can measure the outcome.

Now, let's look at some of the most popular' resolutions often reported. These are taken from various sources and are by no means a completely accurate measure:

- Exercise more
- Lose weight
- Get organised
- Learn a new skill.
- Eat healthier
- Save money
- Get a new job.
- Read more

The lists go on in this fashion. Can you tell why so many people fail?

Many of these aren't specific, measurable, or have time frames attached to them. This makes it difficult to get closer to them in any meaningful way.

New Year Resolution Time

Chapter Five

Resolution Ideas For 2024

Now that you know how to make resolutions that you at least have the possibility of sticking to, you may need some ideas for objectives. We've compiled a list of some initial examples of New Year's resolution ideas below:

- Learn to have a conversation in another language by August by practicing for x hours per week.

- Start by training for at least x hours each month.

- By the end of March, finish an online course to learn the fundamentals of writing Python code.

- Cook one nutritious meal every week throughout the spring to improve your diet.

- Read at least one book a month by committing to read for 30 minutes each night before bed.

- Save x amount each month by setting up a standing order into a separate bank account on the day you get paid.

- Work on your career skills and apply for a new job in a sector you're interested in within the next six months.

You may modify these examples to fit your objectives and way of life, or you can use them as inspiration for something wholly your own. The main thing is that you're committing to a clear action within a specific time frame, with a framework for how you're going to achieve it.

Boost Your Goals for The New Year

Before you even begin to establish commitments for the New Year, individuals often take two typical diversions. Before considering what they really wish to accomplish, they consider what is right to do. Second, they focus on what they ought to give up on instead of what they want to accomplish.

Any change requires a sincere desire on your part to be effective. Make a resolution that you're not really committed to until you take the time to think about what it is that you actually desire.

Since setting goals for the new year is such a well-known custom, they may have significant influence. Everybody is aware that everybody else is organizing. And what a fantastic network for mutual assistance that may provide!

What might separate success from failure is this outside drive and encouragement from yourself and your desire to achieve.

Ideas for New Year's Resolutions and How to Achieve Them

Many individuals are reflecting on their lives and reassessing some of their decisions now that the new year has arrived. For those who haven't started making the changes they promised to start next week, next month, or maybe when winter arrives, the New Year's resolutions provide the ideal chance.

As most individuals don't follow through on their resolutions, now is your time to sit down and develop a list of the main lifestyle changes you want to make. We've chosen to offer you a little assistance because, let's face it, you'll need it.

Chapter Six

Self-Improvements for a Better You for the New Year

Here's a collection of motivational New Year's goals, along with some guidance:

1. Get-in Form

Over one-third of the population wants to lose weight, which is the top resolve among Americans, along with "exercise more" and "stay fit and healthy." Starting a fitness and nutrition program is not too difficult; the challenge is selecting a good one that will provide consistent results and be manageable over time.

Eat better: Make a healthy diet adjustment. Consume a lot of fruits, veggies, and high-fiber meals.

Become more active by signing up for a gym. Try to include exercise into your everyday routines, even if you're too busy. For example, at work, use the stairs rather than the elevator.

2. Consume a Healthier Diet

Usually, this is a continuation of the prior resolution. A better diet may be quite difficult to adopt when inexpensive junk food is all around us. However, you may gradually form healthy eating habits if you put in a fair amount of effort and follow a few simple pointers. Try these nutritious meals, become conscious of your nutrition, and learn to regulate your emotional eating.

Begin by:

Minimize junk food intake: Lower the quantity of junk food you eat. Remove them completely from your diet if at all feasible.

Replace processed foods with fresh ones. Preservatives and excessive salt concentrations are common in processed foods. Make some fresh soup and replace that can of soup.

3. Give Up Postponing

The urge to unwind and do something enjoyable rather than work hard is the main obstacle that prevents the majority of individuals from achieving their objectives. It takes a lot of effort to break the negative habit of procrastination because once you get into it, it's hard to get out of it.

Although there are a lot of helpful strategies available to help you quit procrastinating, the best advice is to divide the task into smaller steps: When we have an excessive amount of work ahead of us, we tend to put it off. Divide the job into manageable chunks and assign due dates to each chunk.

4. Boost Your Focus

For thousands of years, people have been searching for strategies to increase their ability to concentrate and think clearly. The majority of ancient societies used a mix of herbal medication and mental exercises to achieve this objective.

Consider practicing meditation. The mind is trained to concentrate on one subject at a time via meditation. You may improve your attention and focus by meditating.

These days, we may improve our mental abilities and increase our focus by using everything from applications to meditation practices. If you follow through on this, you'll be able to manage your mood, pick things up more quickly, and solve difficulties more easily.

How Well-Sustained Is Your Life?

Use our Time/Life Self-Assessment to determine how balanced your life is and get a free, tailored report.

You'll discover your talents in time management, unearth untapped potential, and take control of your life. Try the free evaluation.

5. Make New Friends

When we find ourselves in a rut, we often wind up spending most of our time at home and miss out on a lot of intriguing possibilities to socialize and network. Don't be scared to go out there and make some acquaintances, since doing so may improve your mental health and advance your career.

Although it might be challenging for shy individuals, this is an excellent resolution for the new year. To begin with, just accept a friend's invitation to go out one evening. This is a really positive first step in getting to know new individuals.

Get out of your comfort zone and engage in conversation with one or two new individuals you meet at the gym or dancing class.

6 Regular Exercise

Some individuals may not even be overweight, and they may even exercise a few times a week, but they spend most of their time sitting down, both at work and at home, which may be detrimental to their health and posture.

If so, all you have to do is figure out how to get up and move about more throughout the day rather than spend it slumped over a computer. If you include friends and family in your hobby, it's much more enjoyable.

Alternatively, you might just start moving. Instead of ordering takeout to be delivered to your house, go for a walk or pace your room.

7. Gain Self-Assurance

Being self-assured makes you more noticeable to others and makes it simpler to ask people out, voice your thoughts, and advance in your career. Having a healthy dose of self-confidence can make your life a lot happier in general.

Having positive self-talk, concentrating on your successes, and seeing failure as a learning opportunity are all part of developing confidence.

Additionally, grin more. You will feel better while you are grinning. You'll feel more certain when you're feeling well.

8. Earn Money to Live Better

Even millionaires are always seeking new methods to increase their income, and the average person could certainly benefit from having a second source of income to live a little more comfortably. Fortunately, there are a lot of possibilities accessible, such as leveraging the internet to your advantage, working as a freelancer, or taking on side tasks.

Think about taking a second job. Look through the internet for possible side gigs and make an effort to establish one.

9. Show More Etiquette

A civilized culture has long placed a high value on having good manners. They facilitate interpersonal connections, help you stay out of trouble, and guarantee that other people think well of you.

Thus, practice good manners, deal with impolite people appropriately, and learn how to say no without offending someone.

Please, excuse me, sorry, thank you, and pardon me more often are the five key phrases.

10. Lessen Tension

This is one of many excellent New Year's goals, as stress is one of the leading killers and may have a devastating impact on your relationships and health. Although it's an inevitable byproduct of our busy contemporary lives, it may be efficiently controlled with the use of practical and simple stress-reduction techniques: How Not to Stress: 10 Strategies for Managing Stress

Plan some "me time" as well so that you may unwind and rejuvenate. It can be for a few hours every day, or it might be a whole day off.

11. Discover How to Be Happy

It is possible to remain miserable even if you have excellent health, a stable income, and manage your stress. Learning to appreciate the little pleasures in life and to keep your spirits up in the face of adversity requires persistence and time.

Expressing thankfulness is a powerful tool for increasing pleasure. To aid in keeping your attention on life's positive aspects, consider keeping a gratitude diary. Jot down three things for which you are thankful at the end of each day.

12. Getting Adequate Sleep

Getting adequate sleep at night may be challenging with all the devices that have flashing lights and blaring warnings, including laptops, cellphones, tablets, huge TVs, and other electronics.

Considering your particular sleep chronotype, you need to acquire enough sleep. Before going to bed, put your devices away for at least an hour. It will be much simpler to fall asleep if you let your thoughts transition into nighttime mode.

Establish a nighttime regimen as well. Set and maintain a consistent bedtime. Every day, try to go to bed and wake up at the same time.

13. Give Up Smoking Cigarettes

Smoking is a horrible habit that many people struggle to break since it not only puts your health at risk but can also drain your bank account. Just be ready to commit a significant amount of willpower to permanently quitting smoking.

Addiction recovery may be very challenging. Seek behavioral treatment, become involved in a support group, or rely on your loved ones.

14. Reduce Your TV Watching

The typical American watches TV for about eight hours a day—more than they do for cooking and most likely for sleeping [3]! That is time that might have been better used for learning, growing, or being physically active. You will become aware of how lengthy and productive a day may really be if you are able to reduce your TV watching time.

15. Continue Reading

Books are a fantastic way to learn a great deal about a wide range of subjects and are also good mental exercises. Finding your favorite kind of book, making time for reading (even if it's just for 10 to 15 minutes a day), and making the habit of reading are the only things needed to finish 20 or more books in a year.

16. Locate a Special Someone

Everyone needs someone to speak to, hug at night, and confide our darkest secrets to, but it takes some trial and error to find the perfect person.

Before we can locate the person with whom we click the most, we need to go out and meet a number of possible mates.

Use these suggestions to ask someone out and have a memorable and unique first date to get motivated on your path to finding love.

17. Enjoy Better Sexual Relations

A significant level of closeness is necessary in every successful relationship, and having sex may really improve our physical and emotional well-being [4]. Making it enjoyable and fulfilling is the goal, and this is something that can be achieved with practice and exercise.

18. Maintain More Orders

It helps to remove the clutter, clean your home, and lead a tidier and more organized life. There are

69

a lot of slobs out there who can't truly keep their things sorted, and a crowded desk or chaotic home can severely affect your productivity and even your mood.

19. Discover How to Wear Style

Your appearance conveys a lot about you, and dressing well may help you seem strong and confident, which can help you acquire a job, advance in your career, and attract the attention of attractive people. Regardless of gender, dress to stand out in a crowd by wearing something that makes you feel good about yourself.

20. Give Important People More Time

We just don't have enough time in this life to spend it on poisonous, deceitful, and dishonest individuals. The greatest method to remain happy and have a satisfying life is to put our attention on the individuals who care deeply about us.

21. Reduce Your Alcohol Consumption

Although consuming one or two servings [5] of any kind of alcoholic beverage per day is perfectly safe and healthy, few individuals can honestly claim to be able to adhere to this recommendation. Although there are many advantages to controlling your drinking, it may be a challenging endeavor.

Begin slowly. If you often have two glasses of wine after work, try cutting that down to just one for a month. After that, consider limiting your consumption to one or two glasses each week.

22. Eliminate Debt

If debt is holding you back in life, it is really impossible to go ahead. Although achieving financial independence is a difficult journey, it is undoubtedly doable with some preparation and self-control. Examine these approaches to debt repayment. It will feel so fantastic that you won't believe it.

23. Saving Money

It's time to start setting money aside after your debt is under control. A rainy-day reserve and some spare cash that may be used for foreign trips, home repairs, or new automobile purchases are refreshing alternatives. Try these effective money-saving strategies.

24. Learn a New Language

Acquiring proficiency in a new language will not only enhance your ability to communicate, but it will also add value to your CV and even lead to career opportunities. There are many sites available these days that let you learn a language for free.

25.Volunteer More and Donate to Charities

Giving your time and effort to those in need is not only a kind deed and one of the really worthwhile New Year's goals, but it's also a chance to network, pick up new skills, and strengthen your CV. Here's how to fit volunteering into your hectic schedule.

25.Develop Useful Skills or Enjoyable Interests

It won't help to just sit around all day. It is much preferable to make productive use of your

Leisure time, learn new skills, and enjoy yourself while doing so. Later on, you'll be glad that you took this action. Whether you're into athletics or communication skills, discover how to pick up new abilities and pastimes quickly.

26.Give Up Resentment

While it may take a lot to overcome hardship and difficult times, moping about ineffectively solves nothing. You will only lose a friend or life partner and stay depressed and resentful if you get into a heated argument with someone and end up upset over a little disagreement. Dealing with difficulties that should be left in the past is much better when done through forgiveness.

27.Get a Pet.

Many individuals who love animals and would be excellent pet owners overthink things, while others simply go out and adopt a pet without realizing the responsibility that comes with it. Make sure you are prepared and choose a pet that complements your way of life and living situation.

28.Organize Yourself Better

No matter how much free time you have, if you can't manage it well, you'll only wind up wasting most of the day circling around. Thus, at the top of your list of New Year's goals should be organization. Organizing yourself will suddenly free up more time, and things will begin to fall into place. Develop the habit, use tools and applications for assistance, and enjoy your newly discovered free time.

29.Take More Trips

Before you contemplate traveling the world, you'll need to get your money in order, acquire the necessary gear, and put in some time and effort. However, there are methods to see distant locations and experience diverse cultures even on a restricted budget.

To satisfy your wanderlust, watch some documentaries, go on a vacation, or exchange letters with a pen friend abroad.

30.Acquire Cooking Skills

One of the most important abilities that any man or woman should have is cooking. It lets you eat the cuisine you love exactly the way you want it, save money, and wow dates with romantic dinners enjoyed by candlelight.

Maintaining your health should be your first concern, but a lot of individuals don't see the doctor as often as they should because they appear afraid of them, sometimes waiting until their illness has become much worse. Regardless of how well you may feel right now, regular examinations are essential.

31. Take a New Look at Yourself

One of your wise New Year's goals should be to make some significant adjustments in your life if you find that no matter what you do, you are never really happy. You may have a whole new outlook on life and go places you may not have thought were possible by reinventing yourself.

32. Quit Being Late

Being punctual is highly valued in our culture; therefore, making this your New Year's goal is a terrific idea. Learn the behaviors of punctual individuals to remain on time. Being on time is a symbol of a genuine professional, a trustworthy friend, and a loving spouse.

33. Become More Independent

We have been somewhat spoiled by technology, a somewhat good government, and companies that provide inexpensive, ready-to-eat food and a plethora of helpful gadgets. As a result, we often reach adulthood without possessing the necessary skills to be independent and self-reliant. Try handling the issue on your own the next time rather than rushing to the closest friend or family member.

34. Make a Career Out of Your Interest

We would all be a lot happier and have a more balanced society if we could all figure out how to combine leisure with work and earn a living doing what we love. While it may not always be feasible, there are instances in which taking up a new pastime might lead to a successful career.

35. Let Go of Your Past

Even if it hurts a lot, it can be preferable to have loved and lost than to have never loved. Although mending a shattered heart is a gradual process, self-care is the first step in surviving this trying period with minimal suffering.

36. Develop Emotional Self-Control

While unchecked rage may lead to many problems, controlling your emotions is an excellent New Year's resolution since feelings like pride and envy can be harmful in any situation. Developing emotional self-control enables you to remain composed and make more logical decisions, even in the face of intense emotional conflict.

37. Be More Responsible

The capacity to consider options before acting is a crucial component of developing into a responsible adult. Just as it's important to safeguard your family and assist in providing for them, it's also critical to accept responsibility for one's actions and refrain from placing the blame elsewhere.

38. Expand Your Knowledge of Culture, Music, And Art

Having a well-rounded education is the best way to blend in while interacting with a diverse range of individuals from various backgrounds. Although many people find it difficult to understand, subjects like history, art, music, and culture may really be rather simple if you take the time to study them.

39. Minimize Your Social Media Time

While some individuals may not spend a lot of time watching TV or playing video games, social media has become a major addiction for people in many different demographic groups. Maintaining relationships with friends and family is OK, but if you find yourself using social media for more than an hour a day, it's time to make a change and put this on your list of worthwhile New Year's goals.

40. Acquire Self-Defense Skills

It's crucial to possess the abilities necessary to protect both your personal safety and the safety of the people you care about. But it's not only about palm strikes and groin kicks. It is essential that you acquire knowledge about proper behavior, both for yourself and others.

41. Embrace Romanticism More

In partnerships that last longer and are more serious, romance often ends up dying first, but it doesn't have to. The romance may last for decades if you only plan date evenings and spend time together. Even if you're not the romantic kind, it will still be enjoyable.

42. Recall Vital Dates

When it comes to romance and maintaining the joy of a committed relationship, you don't want to continually forget milestones like anniversaries and birthdays. You won't ever forget another date again since there are a ton of memory techniques that are easy to learn.

43.Increase Your Social Media Presence

There are benefits to going out and mingling. This is a great New Year's resolution to add to your list since not only can you learn new things, have fun, and meet new people, but you can also hone your leadership abilities and teamwork skills. There are ways to participate pretty actively in a community, even if you are an introvert, very shy, or find it difficult to speak to others.

44.Foster Greater Originality

There are moments when we just lose our creativity due to mental exhaustion. This is especially problematic if your line of work or passion requires you to think creatively and unconventionally. Like everything else, there are many strategies to encourage your creative flow.

45. Use Art to Express Yourself

The majority of us still possess a little creativity, even if some of us are more rational. Making creative expressions of oneself is a fantastic method to relax and maintain mental clarity. You may stay active and burn some calories by participating in some of these activities. Write, create, and do-it-yourself projects—do anything that releases your spirit.

46. Confront Your Insecurities and Fears

This specific point is hidden behind other admirable New Year's promises, but we want to address it since fear and insecurity are often the root of a number of issues. It will help you get rid of a lot of your doubts if you conceive of it as managing and surviving your fear rather than conquering it.

47. Begin Composing a Book Or Journal

You would be shocked at how many individuals there are who would want to share a fascinating tale but lack the courage or writing ability to do so. You should not be frightened to try writing, even if it is simply a few rambling ideas written in a diary every day.

48. Journaling Ideas to Get You Started

49. Adhere to the healthy routines you've established.

The last and most crucial thing to remember is that when you start making healthy New Year's goals, whatever you do for the better must stay. It will take effort to maintain your new, positive habits until they are an inherent part of who you are. That's the path to real self-improvement.

Conclusion

My dedication to personal development goes beyond just making a self-promise to myself this New Year. My ability to think critically and solve problems will improve, both of which are vital in the complicated and dynamic world of today. The benefits are definitely worth the effort, even if the path to accomplishing this resolution is difficult. On New Year's Eve, when the clock strikes midnight, I promise to follow through on my goal and make it a reality in the next year.

As you write your New Year's resolutions, keep in mind that this could be a really good opportunity to better your life, to make sure you are pursuing your dreams, to make sure you aren't wasting time or life as you go through the year, to prevent yourself from feeling like a failure again if that is a pattern for you, and to feel successful as you accomplish your goals and adhere to your resolutions throughout the year.

Seize the chance to create the greatest new year—no, the greatest year of your life. With your essay completed, start in January. Resolve to keep your resolutions at the forefront of your mind all year long (not just the first few weeks of January)? Post it on the fridge, promote it on social media, or do whatever the situation calls for. Subsequently, ensure that you follow through on those intentions.

Bringing Your Resolutions to Fruition This Year!

www.ingramcontent.com/pod-product-compliance
Lightning Source LLC
Chambersburg PA
CBHW060959260726
48661CB00005B/1953